A PROFILE OF PRIVATE SCHOOLS AND PUBLIC SCHOOLS

Basic Information on Public School vs. Private School To Guide You On Selecting The Best School Setting That Will Help Your Child Develop and Excel

Which school can give the best possible education to your child? Do you get him into private school or public school? This is a very basic question, yet very critical decision, any parent is faced with and deliberates on from the time the child is born until he gets to school age.

The only way you can come to a decision and appease yourself that you've decided right for your child is to:

1. Research/make inquiries
2. Study and examine all of the information
3. Evaluate the advantages and disadvantages of each educational system

Both systems can give exemplary education to your child for as long as the child adapts well into the environment he is in. To ensure that he is placed in a school he is well-suited in, as a general guideline, you will need to look carefully into the following areas of consideration:

- Facilities/practical conveniences
- Class size
- Teaching styles/Curriculum
- Financial supply
- Administrative support

Which works best for you and your child? Is the public school system satisfactory enough or do you consider sending him to private school? Read up and make an informed decision.

Table Of Contents

Introduction

One of the toughest decisions that you are going to face as a parent is where to send your children to school.

For a number of parents, the choice of where to send their children for an education is easy do to a lack of options. Many parents have limited time or funds and are unable to even consider sending their children anywhere other than the local public school.

On the other hand, the majority of parents do have the opportunity to consider all available options when it comes to their child's education. If you are having a hard time making the decision to send your child to private school or public school, then you have come to the right place. This book is full of information to help you with making this all-important decision.

In order to select the school that is ideal for your child, you will need to way all of the options that you have available to you realistically. It is important to take into consideration the cost of the school, the amount of time must be invested by the parent, the social impact on your child as well as the specific needs of your child and family.

In the old days, when a child was ready to begin kindergarten, there was a pretty good chance that he or she attended the public school that was just around the corner, or a church school right down the road. For parents back then, deciding which school to send their son or daughter to was an easy task.

The decision is not so simple these days. Education today is more of a compelling and complex topic of discussion across the nation. Questions come up every day in newspapers, homes and political debates about teacher training, school quality, curriculum and accountability.

For you as a parent, this means that in order to choose the best possible school for your child you are going to need to do a little homework of your own. In fact, one of the most important decisions that you make in your child's life is the school to which you send him or her. If you are going to make the right decision, then you must educate yourself by networking, researching and doing whatever it takes to make sure you have a solid understanding of all of the options that are available for your child.

The distinction between private schools and public schools is not as forthright as they were at one time. In fact, in some cases you may find that the local public school in your area is more suited for your son or daughter than a high-class private school with a nationwide reputation and an extortionate price tag. Even though research has been conducted that indicates that private schools often are superior to public schools when it comes to academic programs, this is not always the case.

The gap between private schools and public schools is growing narrower and narrower with each passing day. In spite of the often negative press that public schools receive, it seems that they are actually getting better. Experts agree that if you are looking for a generally all-around good education, a high quality public school may the best option for your child.

However, at the same time, private schools may not be as unaffordable as you think. Take the time to conduct an adequate amount of research to determine all the options that are available to you. Do not rule out private school based solely on your financial situation. Shop around to several different schools and you may be pleasantly surprised.

1

Basic Comparison Between Public Schools And Private Schools

Private schools and public schools both have their own benefits and drawbacks. This chapter covers a few of the most important areas that you must consider when you are looking to make the right decisions regarding your child's education.

No matter if your child is just getting ready to enter school for the first time, or if your child is changing schools for some reason, you need to be aware of all of the choices that you have available to you. It is important to become as well informed as possible so that you will be able to compare all of the prospective schools available to you effectively.

Administration And Licensing

Public schools have administrators known as principals, who must hold a Master's degree in administration. The teachers at public schools must have both a valid teaching license as well as a Bachelor's degree. Many private schools have the same requirements, however, not all of them do.

As you are researching prospective schools, you may be surprised to discover that in some private schools, not all teachers are licensed. This typically happens when a licensed teacher is not available to fill one or more positions in the school. Teacher vacancies in private schools are common due to the fact that the pay at a private school is usually substantially less than that which is paid to public school staff members.

Issues On Behavior Formation

The majority of teachers in the public school systems will agree that the behavioral problems that they must face with their students are getting worse with each passing year. It does seem that the children in public school are becoming more and more difficult to deal with, leading many parents to fear their child will not get the attention they need in a public school to flourish academically.

The teachers in most private schools tell a different tale. Perhaps the reason is that the parents of children in private schools are more involved and willing to pay a little more for a quality education. Maybe there are less behavioral issues among private school students because of the smaller class sizes or uniform requirements. No matter what the reason, private school student tend to be better behaved than children who attend public schools.

In addition, private schools have more freedom when it comes to expelling students. If a child who is attending private school chronically misbehaves, he or she is generally asked to leave the school.

Values Formation

Friendship, patience, loyalty and good citizenship are all character traits that are taught to children who attend public schools. If you choose to send your child to a private school that centers on religion, then a number of Bible courses may also be included in the curriculum, which focuses on memorizing Bible verses, teachings of morality, Bible stories and more. Likewise, Jewish private schools usually teach their students Hebrew, in Catholic private schools the students learn about the saints and so forth and so on. Private schools that are not centered on religion typically offer the same type of character education as most public schools.

Class Size

The teacher to student ration is typically smaller in private schools than in public schools. Especially the smaller church schools, your child will receive more individualized attention at these institutions. Generally, public schools cram as many children as they can legally in every classroom.

In a private school, the classes are so small that on some occasions the students are able to complete the curriculum for the year early and get a head start on the next school year. On the other hand, in some public schools the classes are so large and diverse that some of the material is not taught in the current school year.

Curriculum is not the only concern when it comes to class size. In a school with fewer children, there are fewer children with whom your child will be able to make friends. On the contrary, in a large public school they may disappear into the crowd, which may also limit the number of friendly relationships you child builds during their formative years.

Costs Of Schooling

All public schools are free to attend because they are paid for by taxpayers. The tuition fees to attend private school vary so greatly that it is difficult to estimate overall cost. A number of private schools offer work programs or scholarships to make it possible for children from less fortunate homes the same opportunities. Members of the staff at a private school are typically given the choice of discounted tuition for their children or another type of benefit such as health insurance or assistance with further education.

Curriculum

The curriculum at public schools is mandated by the state. This means that all schools within the state all have the same textbooks and testing requirements.

Private schools are not required by the state to follow the mandated program. Therefore, the tests and textbooks vary a great deal. In a number of the smaller private schools, the curriculum is actually written by the teachers themselves, at least for the most part anyway.

In the larger private schools, the curriculum is typically purchased. The private schools built around religion often opt for textbooks that have somewhat of a religious slant to them. In addition, if the school is seeking accreditation, then some type of standardized testing will most likely be included in the curriculum.

Facilities

Some public schools have facilities that are quite impressive, while others are mediocre at best. The same goes for private schools. When it comes to the public school system, economic revenue base and political support are highly important.

For private schools, the ability to attract donations and other types of financial backing is crucial. The facilities of private schools echo the triumph of the development team as well as the school in order to continue generating support from alumni.

A number of K-12 private schools have amenities and facilities that far surpass those that you might find at many of the universities and colleges across the country. For example, Philips Academy Andover in Andover, Massachusetts, and The Hotchkiss School in Lakeville, Connecticut, has athletic facilities and libraries that closely compare with those of Cornell College and Brown University.

In addition, these schools are able to offer the sports and academic programs that make good use of such valuable resources. You will be hard pressed to find public schools with similar facilities. The do exist, however, but they are few and far between.

Public schools generally reflect the economic status of the surrounding area. Schools in prosperous suburban neighborhoods typically have greater amenities that the inner city schools in urban areas. It just makes sense to assume that a public school in Greenwich, Connecticut, will have more to offer students, as far as niceties, than a public school in Detroit, Michigan.

Fundraising

Both public and private schools have several types of fund raising events in which the students are asked to participate. The fundraisers generally involve the children selling something like candy, magazines subscriptions or wrapping paper.

The majority of private schools tend to go a little farther with their fundraisers than the public schools do, branching out into bake sales, silent auctions and much, much more. Most of the money collected in school fundraisers go to the PTA.

Range Of Opportunities

Public schools generally have more space, more money, more teachers and more overall resources than many private schools have available. Therefore, public schools provide greater opportunities for programs including sports, foreign languages, music, art and more. Private schools typically have to host several fundraisers throughout the year to cover the costs of any additional opportunities that they offer to their students.

On the other hand, private schools offer several different types of opportunities, including more individualized time with teachers, smaller classes and lessons in religion.

Depending on the size of the school, most private schools offer sports outside of school.

Parent Participation

Even though parents are encouraged to volunteer their time at both private and public schools, in many private schools it is actually a requirement. In fact, some private schools have a specific number of hours that each parent is required to spend volunteering for the school.

Versions of a Parent-Teacher Association, or PTA, exist at most private as well as public schools. This organization works as a mediator between the parents and the school. For example, if the school needs money for a new library, they would go to the PTA. The PTA would then work with the parents to determine the best way to raise the funds that the school needs.

Special Services

Public schools typically offer more special services than private schools. If you child requires some sort of special service, such as a learning disability program, counseling, a speech program, or gifted and talented program, then his or her needs may be better met at a public school.

According to law, it is possible for a child to attend a private school and still take advantages of these services that are offered by local public schools. However, it makes more sense to have these services more convenient and readily available by actually enrolling your child in the school that offers the special services that he or she requires.

Teacher Salary And Benefits

All schools would like to pay their teachers the salary that they deserve. However, these days public schools are the closest it gets. In addition to the higher pay, public school teachers are also provided with other benefits, such as insurance plans, retirement plans and plans to assist teachers who wish to further their education.

Teachers at private schools do not enjoy the same salary and benefits as public school teachers. Not only are the salaries less for private school teachers, but they are also denied the benefits of health insurance, retirement packages and other luxuries that public school teachers are able to enjoy. In addition, there are rarely any programs in place for private school teachers interested in furthering their education.

The teachers at private schools are more than happy to do without such amenities for a number of different reasons, including religious views, easier management of smaller, better-behaved classes and tuition breaks for their own children at a high quality educational institution.

Transportation

Bus service is typically available through the public school system. Sometimes, private schools will offer some type of shuttle service from one campus to another, but rarely provide transportation to and from the student's home. However, parents at most private schools are quite organized when it comes to organizing car pools to get their children to and from school.

You have a number of different options from which you can choose when it comes to your child's education. It is important that you take the time to examine all of the options available to you before making any concrete decisions.

Take the time to investigate all of the schools in your area to learn what education options are available for your child. Ask other parents, such as your friends and neighbors how they feel about all the different schools in the area. In addition, it is a good idea to meet with the school administrators in order to determine if the school they run is the one for your son or daughter. Once you have compiled enough information, then you will be ready to make an informed decision about your child's education.

2

The Spotlight On Private Schools

A controversy seems to be increasing across the country with regards to education. Parents everywhere want to know which is best for their child, private school or public school. Many parents are not fully aware of the differences between public and private schools.

The truth is that private schools generally have a lot to offer. In addition, private schools are able to better implement additional programs and employ a higher quality of teachers because of the money that they receive from tuitions, donations and alumni support.

This does not mean that every child would be better off attending a private school. However, if you child seems to be getting lost in the public school shuffle, it may be time to explore the private school alternative.

A smaller number of students attend private schools, reducing the student-teacher ratio to a more manageable number. Most students in an area will attend the local public school. Therefore, public schools are becoming more and more overcrowded. More families today are choosing private schools because the smaller class sizes mean that their children will be able to receive more one-on-one time with the teachers.

The courses that are offered by private schools is usually more accelerated and focused on the things that students planning to attend college will benefit from the most. In public schools, the students are regarded as individuals with different paths that may or may not lead to college following high school graduation. Private schools work based on the philosophy that all of their students will make the natural transition to college, and focus on preparing them for when the time comes to pursue that college career.

In the more well-to-do regions, there may be public schools that have just as much money and are just as focused on getting students to college as most private schools. However, it is in the urban regions where the greatest difference between the two can be seen.

It is important to do your research so that you will be able to make an informed decision about your child's education. When you know all the facts, you will be able to better determine if a private school is right for your child. It is up to you to know your child's particular requirements so you will be able to find a quality school that will be able to meet his or her needs sufficiently.

Incidents with drugs, violence and high school dropouts are less of a problem in private schools. Most likely, this is because of the high level of dedication that the parents of children enrolled in private schools to give their children the best possible future.

Private schools tend to be fairly expensive. However, the powers that be are in talks to create school vouchers that will allow families to use the tax dollars that would normally be spent on the public school system to pay for tuition at a private school.

More and more parents are turning to private schools to protect their children from a public school system that increasingly churns out students who barely scrap by or fail to graduate at all. Generally, private schools are more dedicated to educating children. Choosing the right school is an investment in your child's future, this is not a decision that you should make lightly. Take the time to research all of the school in your area to know what you have available for your children. Then decide if private school is the best choice for your son or daughter.

The Pros And Cons

There are a number of different factors to consider when enrolling your child in a new school, such as location, religion, opportunity, etc. Below are a few common pros and cons of private schools. Keep in mind that all children are unique with unique needs and abilities; be sure to consider all the factors that apply directly to your child.

Deciding to enroll your son or daughter in private school may do away with some of the worry that goes along with traditional public school systems. However, that is not so say that private schools do not have issues of their own.

The Pros Of Enrolling Your Child In Private School

- As a general rule, private schools cost a great deal of money to attend. However, in most cases some type of scholarship is offered to allow students from all types of financial backgrounds the same chance at a quality education. Parents who pay to send their child to a private school often feel that it is money well spent.

- The architecture of private schools is not dictated by cost and functionality. Therefore, most private schools offer a more inviting campus, which provides the students with a higher quality learning environment.

- Private schools are allowed a more selective admissions process. Unlike public schools, private schools are not required to provide an education to all of the children within the surrounding geographical area. The chances are greater that your child will get the attention they need in class if the teacher is not preoccupied by children with behavior problems or other distracting issues.

- Private schools rely of parents a great deal for funding; therefore, they are more eager for face time with the parents. Parental involvement is a welcome benefit to allowing your child to attend private school.

- Private schools have greater control over class size. In a setting that is less frenetic, your child will be able to learn comfortably without the pressures of an overcrowded classroom.

- Unlike public schools, private schools often include religion and morals in their regular curriculums.

- Private schools focused on special missions have a history that is much longer than that of any charter or magnet school. In addition, they also have more experience is their specialties.

- Only certain specialized private schools offer pedagogical approaches to education, such as Waldorf and Montessori.

- Since they do not have to follow any teacher certifications guidelines, private schools are freer to hire a more diverse faculty, including teachers licensed in other countries and teachers with special language skills.

- Even though the pay is not as high for private school teachers as it is for public school teachers, they have more freedom to get creative with their curriculum, which in turns creates a certain loyalty to the school where they teach.

- Private schools are generally geared toward students who are planning to attend college after graduation. Therefore, a superior education is often available.

- Attendance of a private school looks good on an employment resume. Not to mention, all the friends you child will make at private school could prove beneficial in the future as most private school graduates go on to build successful careers.

The Cons Of Enrolling Your Child In Private School

- Enrollment in a high quality private school is not cheap. You can expect to pay a pretty penny to send you child to the best private school. In addition, you will also be expected to pay for a number of different activities all throughout the school year.

- Parents are often expected to play an active role in their child's education by volunteering their time to the school on many different occasions throughout the year. Do not be surprised if you are asked to chaperone a field trip or serve juice at a class party.

- Although many parents are attracted to private schools due to the lack of diversity among the student body, many stay away for the same reason. Parents fear that keeping their child secluded in a school with only other children with the same beliefs and goals will not properly prepare them for the real world.

- Private schools do not have to comply with laws concerning the special needs of students. Therefore, many private schools are not equipped to teach students with special needs.

3

The Spotlight On Public Schools

When the time comes to begin thinking about your child's education, be sure to consider the advantages to enrolling your son or daughter in public school. It is true that public school does have its disadvantages, but a public school may offer the exact education your child needs, especially with the wide variety of extracurricular and academic programs that are usually available.

First of all, an education from the public school system is free to any child of age living in the area. This sometimes means that the value of the academic programs may not be quite as high as what you might find in a private school, however, this is not always the case. If you are looking for a new school because your family is moving, take the time to check with your real estate agent to find out the standard of the schools located in the area to which you are moving.

Classrooms in public schools are typically larger than those that you might find at a private school. This means more students and less one-on-one time with the teachers. However, a high enrolment rate in public schools is not necessarily an all-bad thing.

In a public school, the students are exposed to a wider variety of people from all different types of socio-economic backgrounds. This means that the children who attend public schools often get along better with other people regardless of race, ethnicity, financial background or any other differences. Many parents and experts believe that children who attend public schools are able to experience a more complete education.

The philosophy and terms of curriculum are no surprise in the public school system. All of the public schools must follow the standards that are regulated by the federal and state governments. If you do not wish for any types of religious or theological studies to be included in the curriculum that your child is taught, then public school is the most viable option for you and your children.

Even though violence and dropout rates are typically higher in public schools than in private schools, these statistics do not necessarily include all schools. Take the time to evaluate the educational institutions in your local public school system. Find out how the schools in your area are ranked both nationally as well as statewide to give you a better idea of the programs that are offered. In addition, it is always a good idea to schedule a meeting with the principal of the schools you are considering, and take a tour of the facilities as well. This will allow you to get a better feel for all of the schools in the area so that you are able to make the wisest and most informed decision possible regarding your child's education.

The Pros And Cons Of Public School

Different children have different needs; therefore, it is difficult to pinpoint all of the advantages and disadvantages for all children. Nevertheless, here are some general pros and cons of public schools to get you pointed in the right direction:

The Pros Of Sending Your Child To A Public School

- The number one reason that many parents prefer public schools to private schools is the lack of tuition fees. In fact, a number of school districts around the country even offer transportation to and from school for no charge.

- Many people believe that private schools are reserved for an elite class. Since ninety percent of students in the United States attend public schools, many parents believe that it is an important common experience that must be shared in order to secure democracy. Some parents enroll their children in public schools because they feel that children who attend public school are united as Americans, regardless of race, religion or ethnicity.

- With the growing possibilities for charter and magnet schools within the public school system, many parents feel the same benefits provided by private schools are now accessible without paying high tuition fees.

- Public schools are held to higher standards when it comes to the teachers that they employ. In order for a public school to receive funding from the federal government, all teachers must meet specific certification requirements.

- Although it differs among the various schools, teachers in public schools generally receive better pay and an opportunity to advance in their career.

- Students in public schools spend considerably more time on core subjects, such as social studies, math, science and English. In fact, studies show that public schools spend at least three more hours each week on these subjects than private schools do.

- Public schools are able to host more sponsored activities. When it comes to sports, clubs, learning tools, extra-curricular

27

activities and academic support, public schools have the advantage over private schools. The simple reason is that most public schools are larger, meaning they have the student body necessary to form a computer or glee club. In addition, state and federal regulations insist on public schools providing disability and diagnostic services; therefore, public schools are more likely to offer remedial, talented and gifted programs as well.

The Cons Of Sending Your Child To A Public School

- Many people feel that the education offered at public schools is of lower quality than private schools. Several parents fear the more intelligent children would miss out at public school.

- Peer pressure is often a greater issue in public schools. Students argue with one another on regular basis and learn bad habits.

- The curriculum offered by public schools leaves no room for student individuality, instructor creativity or parental input. In a public school, you child will learn what the school district says they will learn.

4

Deciding Which School System Is Right For Your Child

Once you have a child of your own, you will discover that everyone has an opinion as to where you should send your son or daughter to school. Some people will tell you that the local public schools are the best place for your child, while many others will tell you the only way to ensure a quality education is through private schools.

In order to find the right school for your child, no matter if they are attending kindergarten for the first time or transferring to a new school, you must keep one thing in mind. It is important to remember, your son or daughter is the one who will be going to the school you choose every day. Make sure you chose a school that suits your child by including them in the selection process.

The school that you choose for your child needs to be flexible in order to meet the specific needs of your child on their own level of development. Look for a school that is consistent with your child's particular style of learning and the educational philosophy is one that you find acceptable.

29

Counting Your Child's Opinions

Even if you decide not to completely include your child in the school selection process, you need to talk with him or her at least about the one thing that scares children the most about a new school and that is making new friends.

Although pre-schoolers and children in elementary school are a little nervous about fitting in with a new crowd, middle school and high school children sometimes just flat out panic. Only when you child has developed a confident strategy to make new friends will he or she be ready to move on to all other aspects of a new school.

Before your child starts classes at a new school, you need to provide them with the tools that they need in order to be able to initiate and maintain friendships with the other children in their new school. Knowing how your child interacts with other children is the first step to finding a school that will suit them perfectly. The following are some age appropriate tips to help you with your mission.

Preschool Through Elementary

Even children as young as pre-schoolers often have at least one or two friends in their life. Begin preparing your child for the new school by talking about the friends he or she has already, including how they met, what they like to do together and why they get along so well. Talk about each friendship that is important to your child, emphasizing how they grow.

Talk to your child about how he or she might go about making new friends. For example, if the boy next to them is class has a backpack with the same superhero on it, they may have a few things in common.

Middle School Through High School

The friendships that your child makes in middle and high school will be some of the most important relationships in his or her life. When your child is moving to a new middle or high school, talk with him or her about the friendships that they have had in the past, including any social issues that occurred and the steps that were taken to resolve them. By enumerating past social successes, your son or daughter will gain the confidence necessary to make future friends.

Use your best judgment on how much you want to include your son or daughter in the selection process of the new school. Keep in mind, however, that the more involved he or she is in the school selection process, the greater the stake they will have in the ultimate decision. With older schoolchildren, the involvement should be greater.

Looking Over Probable Schools

The next critical step in determining which school is best for your child is choosing the schools in your area that you plan to visit. You need to limit the number of school visits, as well as entrance exams for your child, to no more than four if your child is going on the visits with you. You do not want your child feeling exhausted from visiting schools and taking tests. If there are more than four schools that peak your interest, then take the time to visit some of them on your own to narrow it down to the top four schools when you take your child along with you. However, as long as you conduct the proper research, you should have no trouble narrowing your list to the top choices. Avoid choosing a school for your child based on reputation alone. Your list should include one school you know you like, two you think you will probably like and one that you do not know if you like or not.

Before you visit any of the public or private schools on your list, you need to request information either through the mail or over the Internet. The majority of schools often have videos, brochures, student visitor days, referral networks and open house events. It is best to visit when school is in session in order to make the most accurate decision.

Before You Visit

It is important to do your homework to ensure you are prepared when you begin visiting potential schools for your child. You need to consider a wide range of critical elements when you are developing ideas about what the ideal school is for your child. The following are some questions that you need to keep with you when you are visiting prospective schools for your child. This list will help you remain focused on your overall goal of finding the school that is best for your child.

- Is that safety of your child at risk at this school?

- Does this school share your educational priorities?

- How many children attend this school?

- What is the student-teacher ratio?

- Is the level of parental communication and involvement satisfactory?

- Which organization oversees the curriculum and instruction of this school?

- What programs are in place for special or gifted children?

- How much are fees for books, labs, supplies, school activities and tuition?

- Where is the school located? What would the commute to and from your home or place of work every day entail? How much do you have to pay for transportation?

Look over these questions often so they are fresh on your mind and take them along with you as you go from school to school looking for the one that is the right fit for your son or daughter.

During Your Visit

When you are walking the halls of a potential school, must pay attention to a few things. The appearance of the school is important. Ask about the security methods that are in place at each school to keep the students physically safe, such as security guards, visitor passes, etc.

You also want to make sure the school is sanitary. Check the cleanliness of the hallways, bathrooms, classrooms and common areas. Finally, you also want to note the level of noise present to determine if the school provides a healthy learning environment.

It is crucial that you visit a potential school at a time when classes are in session. This will make it possible for you to observe the everyday activities and student attitudes firsthand.

Peek in a classroom or two to make sure the size of the classes appear easy for the teachers and staff to manage. Be sure to notice if the students seem to be listening and participating in class or if they are loud and disruptive.

When you are planning your visit to prospective schools for your child, make a special request to meet with some of the students during your visit. As you observe, notice how the children seem to feel about being at school. You want to send your child to a school where the students are happy and love the school that they attend. This signals an environment in which the children make long lasting friendships.

You also want to pay close attention to the teachers at each school. In a well-run institution, the children enjoy and respect their teachers. In return, the teachers treat every child with care, dignity and respect. Notice how the teachers and administrators interact with the students, especially when disciplinary issues arise.

Public Schools Visits

Children who are comfortable in most social situations, confident about their academic skills and overall resilient individuals are likely to do well in public schools. The larger school population and increased class size in combination with such a fast-paced environment may be intimidating for children who are more fearful and less secure.

Typically, public schools do not host special visiting days like many private schools. The majority of the public schools across the country just accommodate potential families all throughout the year. Generally, prospective students are invited to sit in on a class or two while they are in session. In addition, you should be able to arrange meetings with the teachers and the school administrators. Just call the main office of the school and schedule an appointment.

If your son or daughter has special behavioral, emotional, learning or mental disabilities, it is important to evaluate the special needs programs at each of the schools that you visit. The federal law, the Individuals with Disabilities Act of 1975, states that all public schools must provide such services to qualifying families free of charge.

If you are not sure if your child requires any special services, there are steps that you can take in order to ensure your son or daughter gets what they need from their education. There is a process where the parents, student, teachers, school counselors and administrators meet in order to evaluate and identify a student's particular educational needs. Once this process is complete, qualifying students are provided with a wide-ranging system of support, including special classes, special programs and even a personal aid if necessary. The results and conclusions of this testing process can be revised and reviewed at the request of the student's parents.

A number of families are taking advantage of assistance from education advocates and private educational diagnosticians in order to have support through the complicated process of ensuring your child, no matter what needs he or she has, receives the best education possible. If you need special services for your child, do not hesitate to contact the school that you are considering. You should be able to get information about the special education department, such as contact information and admissions and testing requirements.

Private School Visits

Most private schools pride themselves on providing smaller classes, more one-on-one time with teachers and an overall quality education. However, private schools, unlike public schools, are not mandated by the federal government to accommodate children with all types of needs. Do not assume that just because you pay for private school that they will provide everything your child needs. Be sure to ask each school about any special programs and services that they provide.

It is best to start your private school visits at least one year before your child is to enroll. A lot of private schools host some type of open house event in the fall, highlighting the academic, athletic and other programs available. In addition, you will most likely be able to take a tour of the school you are considering for your child during such events.

Admissions personal are usually on hand during these events to answer any questions or begin the admissions process.

Most private schools charge a fee to submit an application for admission, which generally ranges anywhere from $25 to more than $100. In addition, the majority of private schools will require your child to take a test such as the Wechsler Intelligence Scale for Children, which is a psycho-educational battery. More and more private schools are requiring students entering grades five through eleven to pass the Secondary School Admissions Test. You can find more information on both the WISC and the SSAT online. Be sure to ask the private school you are considering about any testing fees and locations before your visit.

The tuition to attend an independent private school varies from as little as $120 each month for your child to attend preschool twice a week to as much as $4,000 every month for your child to attend a private high school for students who have severe mental, social or emotional disorders or some type of substance addiction. Annual tuition to attend a Catholic archdiocesan private school is usually $2,500 or less.

The majority of private schools have some type of scholarship or financial aid program in place for students who qualify. Remember to ask up front about the available programs. You should be able to apply for financial aid when you submit your initial application for admission. Keep in mind that grants are limited and present students are generally favored for receiving funds over new or transferring students.

In some school districts, vouchers are available. With a combination of these vouchers and the financial aid programs that are already in place, you should be able to reduce the high cost of private school tuition to something that is more on the level of your family's particular income. Contact the department of education in your state to find out if these valuable vouchers are available in your area.

Level Of Parental Involvement

The level of parental involvement varies from one school to the next. Some private schools require that each student's parents volunteer a minimum number of hours to the school throughout the year.

Most schools, both public and private have some sort of PTA or Parent-Teacher Organization in place. You should be able to get most information about parental involvement from this group.

When you are considering a school, you need to find out the ways in which the parents are encouraged to participate in their child's education. Take the time to find out how active the PTA is and what type of relationship the organization has with the school. Make it a point to find out about recurring issues on which the PTA focuses primarily.

Program Of Study And Testing

The majority of public schools make the curriculum and testing results available online at either the school district or state websites. All of the public schools in the country are provided with an official ranking by the United States Department of Education.

A great number of the private schools across the country have been granted accreditation from the national Association of Independent Schools. In order to receive such accreditation, private schools must undergo a laborious process of evaluation.

Any school to which you are considering sending your child should be more than happy to provide you with information regarding testing, accreditation and government ranking. If this data is not readily handed over by the school, then this is not the school for your child and it would be in your best interest to continue with your search.

Here are so questions that you should answer about each school before filling out any applications for admission or other enrollment forms:

- How is this particular school ranked on the state and federal indexes?

- If it is a private school, is it properly accredited by a reputable organization such as NAIS?

- What are the most recent test results for the school?

- Is there a required entrance exam?

- What are the requirements for graduation?

- Are there any advanced academic or special education programs in place?

- Are there programs that encourage and recognize individual achievement and creativity?

- Are music, art and physical activity included as part of the regular curriculum, or are programs for such in place?

Evaluation Procedure

When you are trying to determine which school is the best one for your child, it is important to ask each potential school about their process of evaluation. Ask what types of reports are provided by the teacher, what type of grading standards the school follows as well as how student progress is reported to the parents.

For each school that you consider, make sure to find out about meeting with your son or daughter's teacher. You need to ask if the school offers regular teacher conferences or if they are at least available upon request from a student's parents.

Especially if your child has had academic issues in the past, you want to learn about each school's early warning system for any problems that may arise with your child academically. You need to know if the teacher will send home some sort of notice or letter of concern should your child develop any problems keeping up with the regular lessons.

Another option that many schools these days offer is tutoring. Some schools have a tutoring system in place to help students who are struggling academically, while others will direct you to students and teachers who provide such services on their own time. Find out what the school offers in regards to tutoring services and be sure to ask about any fees that may apply for such services.

School Fees And Expenses

When you are evaluating educational institutions for your child, it is important to keep your eyes and ears open so that you are aware of all of the fees you will be expected to pay in order for your child to attend. This applies to both private and public schools. It is crucial that you pay attention to avoid the unwelcome surprise of any unbudgeted expenses.

When you first contact each school, you need to obtain an estimate of how much it will cost to send you child to that school for an entire year. Be sure to ask if the estimate you receive includes any extra fees for labs, gym class or books. These questions are some that you need to ask at both private and public schools.

Be sure to ask about sports and any other extracurricular activities that may be offered at the school. You need to find out the costs that are involved in order for your child to participate. In addition, you also need to find out if transportation to and from extracurricular events, such as games, meets, etc., is provided and if there is any cost to you for the services provided.

Feeder Schools

A feeder school is one that produces a noteworthy number of graduates who continue to study at a specific school, or even in a specific industry. Feeder schools are often found in the larger school districts, where the majority of graduates of many of the primary schools all attend the same middle school. On the high school level, you will find there are a number of college preparatory schools that feed the local universities in an area.

When you know which schools in an area feed into which other schools, you will be able to ensure that the education that you son or daughter receives is consistent. In addition, you will also be able to make sure that he or she stays on the right track toward a successfully college experience or specialized vocation in the future.

The greater an idea you have of the community that is feeding into a school, the better you will be able to determine whether or not the school that you are considering is going to meet your child's educational needs and support your ideas and goals as well. Be sure to discuss this topic with the administrators of the school when you are planning to visit the schools on your list.

Here are a few questions that you may want to ask about feeder schools in your area:

- Which schools do most of the students attend before and after this particular school?

- What is the percentage of students that graduate from this school and go on to college, and which colleges do they usually attend?

- Does the school have a favorable reputation among the colleges in the area?

School Placement Counselors

If the task of tracking down the ideal school for your son or daughter sounds like one that you would rather not tackle, then you have options. You can hire a professional to help you get the job done. As private schools are becoming more and more popular and accessible, more and more parents are turning to professional independent school counselors and school placement counselors to ensure the best possible education for their children.

Through student evaluations and interviews with the family, school placement counselors help parents choose the educational institution that is best for their child. They use the information that they learn and the data that they collect to find a school that suits the specific needs and talents of the child in question to find the most appropriate schools.

Some professional school placement counselors also act as an authorized testing center for some private schools and provide entrance testing. Independent school counselors are certified by the Independent Education Consultants Association. The most experienced receive the title of Certified Educational Planner.

The great thing about using an independent school counselor is that the typically have personal knowledge about all of the schools that they recommend. In fact, professional school placement counselors generally spend a minimum of twenty-five percent or more of their time spending time at the schools in the area and developing valuable relationships with the staff and administration.

Most of the time, the professional school placement counselor will conduct the process of application for the most favored schools. A counselor who is well established in their field will be well known by the schools in the area. Therefore, you should be able to get a few recommendations for respected counselors who are willing to do what it takes to secure your son or daughter's spot in the best possible schools.

The downside, however, is that hiring the services of a professional school placement counselor can be quite a costly venture. The fee for these services is paid by the individual clients, not the schools. This fee may range anywhere from as low as $75 for standardize testing to more than $2,500 for the complete package, including placement in some type of therapeutic program.

Take the time to shop around and explore your option before you hire a school placement counselor. Ask around at schools and other parents to get recommendations. If you hire a counselor that was recommended by the quality institution you wish for your child to attend, the counselor will know for sure what the particular school is looking for in their students. By enlisting their services, you will have the upper hand in securing the best possible education for your child.

5

A Focus On Special Issues

Whether a public school or private school is deemed as the right educational system for the child, every parent will be called on to weigh up matters that will pertain to the overall formation of the child's character not only for personal edification but including moral values, social interaction and spiritual development so that the child comes out to be a well-balanced individual to himself personally as well as to the society he is a part of.

Each child is different, with needs and requirements dissimilar to one other. The environment he will be placed in, day in and day out, will play a very large part on what he assimilates and, consequently, what he becomes eventually in life. If the child fits in well into his environment, all his natural instinct to develop and grow is nurtured.

This section will help you look at special issues concerning children's education present in both the public and private school systems.

A Place For The Gifted Child

When you recognize that your child is gifted in some particular area of talent or intellect, getting the school system to recognize that special ability can be a challenge. For the most part public schools are designed to accommodate the "normal" range of children. Because it' a legal requirement not only that you send your child to school but that the state provides public schools to meet that need, most of the children in public school are neither gifted nor special needs.

As such the majority of the resources and the skills of the teachers are built around the need to teach large classes of average students. There is nothing wrong with this approach as our society depends on good education for everybody. But what this does mean is that public schools simply are not oriented toward providing specialized classes for gifted students.

Now there are gifted programs in most schools which offer classes that are "accelerated". This means the curriculum is more challenging and difficult so the student conquers a harder work load then other kids in their grade level. But if you look at this approach closely, this is not really a program for gifted children. These are classes for highly intelligent students or kids who are exceptionally good at learning so they will be the ones to earn scholarships to college.

49

But very often truly gifted students do very poorly in these kinds of classes. That is because often when a child has a particular area of excellence, that does not mean the child is gifted in all areas of academics. So your child might be a brilliant musician, mathematician, chess player or dancer but in every other way average in his or her ability to handle the routine workload of school.

The outcome of putting such students into gifted programs is (a) they don't get specialized training in their particular gifts and (b) they do poorly in accelerated programs which results in poor self esteem and bad report cards which disguise the true genius of this child. These problems with how public schools handle gifted kids point to the need for you to look into finding private instruction that can design a program to take your child to the next level in his or her area of specialization while teaching the other academic subjects in ways that the child can excel in every endeavor at school.

Private schools can provide the focus on your child's particular area of excellence simply because they are private and they don't have the burden of providing education for everybody. Specialized training needs the services of specialized teachers who themselves are outstanding in that field of study or in your child's gifted area. So if your son or daughter is a phenomenal talent in playing the violin, you need violin teachers who can bring that talent along and knows how to take that talent to the next level and the next and the next.

50

Private schools can afford to keep such gifted teachers on staff. They can also afford to have any specialized tools or equipment that is needed to help your child develop his or her gift. Further, the field of excellence your child will develop has a path to success that is unlike the paths most kids take to state college and beyond. Your child may need to seek specialized education beyond high school that takes recommendations and a resume that a private school can help your youngster develop.

The private school setting can tailor your child's curriculum so all of the routine academics can be taken care of but there is plenty of time for your boy or girl to focus on their gift under the tender loving care of a skilled professional. These gifted teachers can become mentors to your child to show him or the path toward success and greatness in the particular area of genius where your child is gifted.

These are compelling reasons to find the perfect setting that will polish and bring out the talent or gift in your gifted child. It might be more expensive but if investing in top notch education for your youngster means that he or she genuinely realizes that tremendous potential, its worth whatever it takes to make that happen.

Child Safety & Protection

There are a lot of reasons that parents consider pulling their kids out of public schools and putting them in private institutions. The quality of education and lower teacher to student ratios often are sited. Private schools can do better with special needs or working with students with special talents as well. But by far the biggest reason for the exodus from public schools is the issue of drugs and violence in public school settings.

There have been plenty of movies that focus on gang life in high schools and the influence of adverse peer pressure that your child might undergo if exposed to negative elements at school. But oddly enough, the Hollywood representation of the influence of drugs and violence in public schools understates the case rather than overemphasizes it. To be blunt, the influence of drug cultures and of violent individuals can easily cause profound changes in your child and changes that are far from what you want for your offspring.

As parents, we want our children to mix with other kids with the same values and children who have ambition and good goals in life so the good teaching you have given to your kids in childhood can come to a good fruit in their teen years. Unfortunately, in many public schools, kids who are not there for education but have other agendas including illicit sex, drugs, criminal activity or violence are often seen as heroes and emulated by other kids. It is very easy for your child to fall in with the wrong kids in such a place and go down the wrong path before you have a chance to stop it.

The tragic stories of such things happening are far too common and they break the heart of any parent who wants only the best for his or her child. Some of the fault comes from the fact that the law requires that the state and city support public education for every child in the community. That naturally means that your child will be in classes with people who could have a negative influence on him or her. It is literally a place where you cannot protect your child and a place where even if your child has strong values and resists the influence of the drug culture and the temptations offered there, they still could become a victim of random violence that occurs frequently in such schools.

Despite the large public education budgets we read about in the papers, public schools are always chronically under funded. That means that classes are too large and teachers are often unable to control antisocial behavior in class. The worst outcome of such an explosive situation is violent outbursts where people get hurt or worse. At the very least this kind of setting makes a quality education virtually impossible and your child will come home traumatized and just glad to have survived the day rather than coming home happy and challenged academically.

In the last few years, large scale school shootings have made our concern for the safety of children at public school an even bigger concern. Yes, schools have responded with tighter security and more efforts to keep students intent on killing others from reaching your kids. But it is a public situation and the continued incidence of school shootings shows that even high security measures can only go so far.

These dangers make private school an attractive alternative. While even at the private school level, security is not guaranteed, the smaller community can do more to know the students well, counsel those who are troubled and build the kind of community that discourages the influence of drugs and violence. And that is the kind of educational setting we all want for our kids.

Drugs In The School System

Anyone who has an interest in what is going on in the world of children's health has noticed the explosion of medications and diagnosis of children with ADD, ADHD, Asperger syndrome or Autism. Does is strike you as strange that all of a sudden a huge percentage of otherwise normal and healthy children are being diagnosed with these dire diseases and schools and their associated medical counterparts are prescribing all manner of strange sounding drugs to "fix" these problems?

When we were growing up, just because a kid didn't sit still in class, the teacher didn't scream that the child had some disease and demand that he be drugged. But that is exactly what is happening to thousands of children in public schools all over this country. And at some point, it's up to parents to stand up and say, "STOP. You are not going to keep pumping drugs into our kids just because you can't control your classrooms."

If you were to make that kind of statement to a school on behalf of your own child, you would face tremendous amount of pressure to have your child tested medically for one of these "behavioral diseases" so the medical community can cooperate with the schools and prescribe Ritalin, Concerta, Paxel or one of the other common behavior control drugs. Schools have a fair amount of leverage over us when it comes to forcing us to drug up our kids. Because these diagnoses are supposedly backed up by medical experts, the schools can maintain that you must comply and get your child on medication or be guilty of child neglect or abuse.

Because you are required by law to have your child in school, the school knows that the threat of holding a child back, expelling them or putting them in special needs classes each holds a terror that works very well at getting parents to play along with their plan. Now this is not to say that there are no children who are not good candidates for such medication. But the use of these drugs is be pushed for such a big percentage of children that its easy to see that what is going on here is nothing short of criminal.

There are plenty of reasons to believe that neither the schools nor the medical "experts" who peddle these drugs are being objective about what your child really needs. One big clue that your child is not a chronic problem is if he or she is perfectly happy and social at home and the problems only occur at the school. That tells you that the problem is with the school, not with your child.

We teach our kids to say no to drugs. So it's about time we also taught our schools to say no to the idea of drugging up our kids just so they are more pliant in the classroom. The first thing to do is to take the teeth out of their threats to hold your child back or otherwise punish you or your child. And that can be done by researching your private school options.

It might sound harsh but unless your child's pediatrician that you know and trust have independently diagnosed your child with one of these behavioral problems, the minute the school tries to put that label on your child, it might be time to go. The last thing you want is to give the public school the leverage to threaten you and try to get away with it.

And if they begin to loose students because of these threats, maybe they will get the message that parents don't want their kids pumped full of drugs and that we want our children to learn with all of their mental and emotional faculties fully alive each and every day of their lives.

Dealing With Becoming A Snob

When you talk to a lot of parents, its amazing how many consider the public school system to be the only option for getting a quality education for their children. It seems that this limited view of education would have fallen by the wayside by now with so many options for getting your kids through school. But that is how effective the government sponsored public schools have been at maintaining the myth that they are the only way to go and that public school is the end all and be all of education for kids like yours and mine.

When it comes to private school, there is another myth or misconception that we would do well with dumping. And that is the image of private school being only for the super rich and that they are full of snooty prep school girls and boys who are dropped off by chauffeurs and spend their summers in the south of France. This concept that to move your child to a private school somehow makes you a "snob" is worth discarding so that all of us can have options to consider rather than being trapped into the tyranny of enduring whatever the public school system tell us we must endure.

All you have to do to overcome this conception you might have that you have to be a snob to take advantage of private schools is take a day and visit a handful of schools in your area. You will find that the variety and diversity of schools is truly amazing. But more importantly, you will see that the kids in private schools are just like your kids, that the cars their moms and dads drive are the same kind you drive and that ordinary people just like you and I take advantage of the higher quality education and the better educational experience that is available for kids in private school.

Whether or not you keep your kids in public school or send them to private school should not be a matter of economic status or whether you fit in any particular social circle. While there are many good things about public school, the fact is that public school is not for every child and not a good fit to the educational goals of every family. And if you did take some time to visit several popular private schools in your area, you may find that there are kids of families you know using those facilities and kids who would provide a good peer group for your child if you did move her to a private facility for the next phase of her education.

We tend to view private schools as being the enemy of public school but that is also to some extent a myth. In a lot of way private schools is an excellent supplement to provide high quality educational options for certain niche students that the public schools cannot serve as well. Public school is, after all, an institution set up to serve the entire community of school age children. This is a big challenge so the school administration has to put the majority of their resources and energies into managing the education of for that large group of "average" students.

But many students benefit from the smaller environment and from specialized skills and focus areas that private schools can afford to take care of. This includes children with special needs such as educational or physical challenges. But it also includes children who are high achievers in certain areas such as the sciences, mathematics or the performing arts. Private schools can also provide an isolated environment for families who want an education built around faith based curriculum which is just not possible in a public school setting.

So there is no reason to shy away from considering private school along with all of your other educational options for your child. If you do consider private school and then decide to take advantage of the services they offer, you are joining thousands of other families who are benefiting from the diversity of educational options we have at our disposal today. And in doing so, you are in

59

no way becoming a "snob". You are just being a good parent by giving your child the best education possible. And nobody would fault you for that noble desire.

Changing Schools - Your Child's Viewpoint

There is one thing that is a bit strange about the process we, go through to pick the right school for our children. Parents often develop a very systematic evaluation system for picking a school which weighs the academic resources of the school, the abilities of the teachers, the schools physical plant and how classes are organized. Often the schools "mission statement" is taken into account on the theory that if the school was founded on certain basic principles, you should see those principles in action at the school.

But even after we go through that systematic process, we have left out one big factor which how your child will feel about the prospect of going to this new school. After all, even if the new school looks great on paper and passes all of your requirements, you are not the one who will have to live at that school spending almost as much time there as at home. So if your child isn't happy with the new school, no matter how great their computer lab is or how qualified the math teacher is, there is a chance of failure.

Probably the one thing you can do to help your child make the adjustment to the new school is to give her a vote in the choosing of the new school. The odds are that you are looking at changing schools for a reason, particularly if you are moving your child from public to private school. So if there are negatives at the old school, your child knows about them. Discuss the option of changing schools and weigh that big change against staying in the current school system and putting up with the faults there.

But keep the door open to the possibility and make the search for a better school a family project. Let the student in the family who will be most affected look at the check list of questions and the selection criteria for the new school and make additions and changes. By giving the child ownership in the selection process, he or she will be much more excited about making the move when the time comes.

You can go on the initial interview at the schools yourself so you can take your time and ask the "adult" questions before your child gets involved. But after you narrow down the choices by weeding out the schools that you say "no way" to, bring your son or daughter on the second visit. Your child can ask more questions and to visit classrooms and meet teachers which will give your child the chance to visualize life at that school. This engages the youth in the process so he or she is excited about the adventure of the big change rather than feel that you are forcing that change without regard for his or her feelings.

One of the biggest concerns your son or daughter will have will be about leaving friends behind and going to a school where they don't know anybody. By starting early and visiting the school often, your son or daughter can identify some people in the school that they do know so they are not totally isolated when they get there. And when they see that private schools have some very creative and often much better funded clubs and special activity groups to get involved with outside of class, that excitement can really begin to grow.

Transition to a new school is hard. But by letting your kid be part of the process and even having him or her sit in on a day of classes, the anxiety of that change will go down. And when the excitement of the change goes up, you will have made a big step forward in assuring this change of schools experiment will be a big success.

The Issue Of God

It has not always been a problem to have a religious faith and still attend public school. But in some ways, that task has gotten more difficult in the last few years. Now people of faith are used to living in a world where there are a lot of different religious points of view. That leads to conflict, discussion and interaction between peoples of various belief systems and that is healthy.

But in the last few years, it seems that there have been a lot of different interpretations of The First Amendment. It seems that as many people see that part of our founding documents as being a rule that dictates freedom FROM religion as much as it does freedom OF religion.

So the question that must be confronted is not whether your child can live in a secular school where there are people who don't like religion or have other faiths. But that is part of training your child for life to be able to be who they are which might be different from whom other people are. The real issue is whether at the administrative level schools are becoming more oppressive so much so that people of faith are being forced to go "into the closet" and hide their values and their religious beliefs.

From the perspective of a parent of a family of faith, the decision about whether to try to work it out with the public school system so your kids can enjoy all the benefits of public school and still maintain their faith with some integrity versus going down the private school route is a tough one. Large public schools do have much more diverse programs and better facilities than small faith based private schools can afford. A big public school often has very well developed physical education, sports programs and gym facilities. The academic diversity is stronger because there are so many more students to offer courses for.

These are all big pluses for your kids. And kids don't always like the idea of being separated from the rest of the population just because they have a religious faith like they were lepers or somehow not acceptable because of their religion. But that is the message that is often passed to youth who not only are devout in their beliefs but live those beliefs out without shame.

To even have a religious study or prayer time at school is often attacked as somehow violating the separation of church and state. Of course anyone who understands that part of our legal system knows that The First Amendment simply restricts congress from passing laws that violate that separation. There is nothing in The First Amendment that says that individual citizens cannot be people of faith and that they cannot openly exercise their faith. In fact, that is what The First Amendment was written to protect.

There are some values to moving your kids to religious based private schools to consider as well. These kinds of schools often offer a good variety of faith based classes where your child can get credit for studying religious documents or learning elements of the faith such as worship or religious music studies. And because the school is private, prayer and open exercise of the religion is not only encouraged, it is included in the curriculum in the classroom, at assembles and in every aspect of school life. Your kids may be able to enjoy a school experience with other kids from their temple or church and not face all of that conflict that becomes so tiresome in the public school setting.

So it's a decision that will take some thought, prayer and discussion. But you do have options about the lifestyle you want your kids to experience in their school lives. And it's always good to have options.

The Dilemma of Finding a Good Christian School

Christian people often feel a bit isolated in society. And for a Christian family, the decision about how to raise your children to be strong in the faith but still able to function in a world full of people of many religious views is a constant challenge. Probably one of the biggest decisions you may have to make that will have far ranging implications on the way your kids interact with the world and how they view their faith is whether to let them go to public school or take the step of putting them in a quality Christian private school where they can exercise their faith openly and without fear of ridicule or limitations.

Christian parents are no different than any other mom and dad who are seeking nothing but the best for their kids. And when evaluating schools, the quality of education has to be the top consideration. Many times public schools do offer top notch programs simply because large public schools can afford to offer diverse programs and a strong curriculum of support activities including sports, theater and the arts. And if your son is gifted in basketball, football or swimming, many times public school is the only option if he has aspirations to work professionally in this field of athletics that God has gifted him.

Socially your kids may also prefer to go to public school for the simple reason that many of their friends go there and to sequester them into a Christian private school may separate them from friends they have known for many years. Having a strong support group and peer network is one of the big factors that makes many young people happy and productive in their school environment. It is not unlikely that even other church kids with whom your child has grown close may be opting for public school because of the strength of the programs, not to mention the reduced costs to their parents.

From a faith perspective, there is something to be said for allowing your kids to mix with students of many faiths or with students that have no religious affiliation at all. It is part of the Christian calling to be of a positive influence in the world and if your kids are strong in their faith and the joy of being raised with a strong faith comes out in their personalities, that can be a draw to Christianity for other kids who would benefit from the loving culture and the strong religious teaching your church offers. So the "evangelistic" considerations of keeping your kids "in the world" might also influence your decision on where they should go to school.

The extent to which your child can exercise his or her faith at the school without fear of intimidation or harassment is also a factor in this decision. The culture of many public schools allows freedom of religion so the Christian kids can meet for bible study and prayer just as much as the children of other religions are welcome to gather and celebrate their faiths freely and in public as well. If this is the setting in your town's public schools, your kids may be able to abide peacefully in that community without difficulty.

However, some communities and the public school cultures in those communities have become hostile to religious expression of any sort. You see how that plays out in a lot of schools where it gets so out of hand that students are actually prosecuted for simply gathering in a public space to discuss their faith or pray. This is not in truth a violation of the separation of church and state guidelines in the First Amendment but these communities use that concept to harass Christian kids. And if that is the culture at the public school level, that may begin the exodus of many Christian kids, including yours to quality Christian private schools in your area.

Of course when considering that shift, the Christian private schools must also measure up academically and foster a culture where children of many denominations can gather and celebrate their shared faith equally and joyfully. But in such a school, prayer can be part of the daily life of class, bible study part of the curriculum and worship included in all assemblies. And this can be a tremendous blessing to your kids when they can enjoy their faith fully even while at school.

Taking Control of Moral Education

People remove their children from public school and move to private schools for a lot of reasons. For one thing, the contract you have with a private school is in every way different than your relationship with public school. Because you pick your private school, the schools in your area are in competition for your "business". That means they work for you and they are responsible to live up to their promises to you when you pay them to give your child an education.

This phase of the process, when you are interviewing various private schools is when you have the chance to stipulate exactly what part of the education of your child you are prepared to hand over to the school and what parts you do not want them fooling around with. For most parents, we are looking to send the child to school go learn about history, English, science, math, foreign language art, composition and other academic subjects that they need to conquer to be a success in college and eventually in life.

Unfortunately public schools also take it upon themselves to educate children in what might be considered moral, ethical or even religious areas of life. And for many parents, this is meddling and imposing values on their children that the school has no right to impose and that is outside their authorization to do so. No other subject better illustrates this principle than sex education.

Sex education in schools is a topic of considerable controversy. And it will continue to be controversial because it is something most parents do not want to see the schools getting involved with and something most schools very much want to have as part of their curriculum. The grey area comes in the realm of physical education. Lessons on hygiene, anatomy and how the human body works are a natural part of the science or physical education curriculum. So you might be able to understand if part of that education is to go over how the human sex organs work from a scientific point of view.

Even at this basic level, though, parents often feel they should be consulted on what they want their children to know. The age old image of dad sitting on the porch and explaining the birds and the bees to his son is time honored and revered in families and we are as a society not comfortable with handing that job over to some stranger whose values we know nothing about.

But sex education in schools doesn't usually end with a basic discussion of the medical of physical properties of the body. Many schools have more advanced curriculum that cover the sex act, how pregnancy works, venereal disease and "recreational" sex activities as well in some cases. And some of the more aggressive programs actually provide condoms to the children "just in case."

You may become alarmed at any or all of this level of instruction if it is to be considered part of a public school's educational program. The problem is because our contract with public schools gives no control to parents, you only have the choice of be quiet and let them teach what they will or remove your child to move to a private school who is more prepared to regard the parent's wishes in regards to sex education or any other areas of moral, ethical or religious education that they wish to carry out at home.

If these kinds of programs at the public school level are what have alarmed you and began your transition to become a private school family, you are not alone. And maybe if enough families go this route, the public schools will get the message that parents have rights in these matters and those rights must be respected.

When Fear Is Part Of School Life

You can probably think back on some of your favorite classes when you was growing up and going to school. And when you think back fondly on that class, how would you describe the atmosphere of the class and the motivation system that was used by the school and by the administration to get you to achieve and excel? The odds are if that class is one you remember as inspirational and one of the favorite times you had in school, the relationship with the teacher was relaxed, creative and affectionate. And the one emotion that you no doubt never felt in that classroom was fear.

We brought this topic up with that illustration because it is really amazing how often fear is the center of the culture at many schools where the objective is to inspire students to learn. This is particularly true in public schools. The culture of public schools very often becomes overwhelmed with the need for order and the strict stipulations for student attendance and tracking put on the school by state regulations. The outcome is the administration of the school often lives in fear of failing in one of these many state level requirements for fear of losing funding or some other form of punishment. And that fear is passed along to the students.

71

Fear is also a culture of a school that is overcrowded. The simple fact is that even if the teacher of a particular course is creative and loves being with students and filling their minds with the joy of learning, if you overwhelm that teacher with more students than he or she should reasonably have in class, the emphasis of the classroom shifts from learning to keeping order. And when that change of priority takes place, fear is the primary tool used to maintain order so the information can be presented to the students.

Sadly, if students are in that room after being intimidated and threatened, even the best of student will close his or her mind to learning. If you are a parent and you sit in on a class to see how well the craft of teaching is carried out, you come away with the misperception that the class was well run if the students sit quietly staring forward while the teacher lays out bland information for them to adsorb and write down. If young people sit quietly and do not interact with the teacher, they are doing so out of fear. And fear is one of the worst teaching tools there is.

Private schools have the opportunity to create a better learning environment for their students because traditionally private schools have a lower teacher to student ratio so interaction is encouraged and fear is not needed to maintain order in the classroom. But even then to foster an atmosphere of discussion and learning, you must have teachers who are talented at leading group discussions, who write their curriculums to include interaction as a teaching tool and who are not afraid of the students.

Fear goes two ways in a school situation. If the student body is frightening to ach other, very often they are also frightening to the teachers. This is the setting where gangs develop in school cultures or where the culture of student life deteriorates to where troubled students can impose fear on others. In this day and age of school shootings and other violence related campus outbreaks, if the school allows that kind of culture to grow up, it is very difficult to get it under control. And just as fear from the top down destroys the love of learning, fear from the student body up destroys a teachers ability to communicate his or her love of the subject matter openly and leads to dull and uninteresting classrooms which only makes matters worse.

As with controlling fear due to overcrowding, private schools also have the edge in controlling fear coming from the student body. Private schools are not required to keep any students that they don't feel fit the culture of the school. Each and every parent and student sign contracts agreeing not to become disruptive in action, dress or attitude and what is disruptive are left to the school to determine. So private schools can remove students who are a threat and with their removal, the fear of harm goes as well.

The Rights Of Parents

Sometimes it seems that once you drop your children off at the door of the school that your rights as parents seem to disappear. This is one of the most disturbing things about sending your child off to school and to public school in particular. In many subtle ways, the school seems to send the message to you that you should go home and bake cookies and not meddle in what is going on in that school. And many parents just blindly accept that implied relationship as long as the children come home relatively happy and seem to be passing so they can move on to the next grade.

But we, as parents, must remember that at no time does anyone have the ability to take away your right to know what is going on with your child and what he or she is being taught. You gave birth to those children and pour all of your love and caring into them so they will be able to reflect your values and grow into good, responsible people with the values of their parents.

Just because it's time for the kids to go to public school, all of that caring and parenting you put in doesn't go out the door. We do not live in a dictatorial state where we turn over our kids to the state to be raised to be good little soldiers and echo whatever state driven dogma they are being taught at school. And while this depiction of what goes on at school is a bit harsh and overly dramatic, you do have the right to question what is being taught at your children's schools and object to any "indoctrination" that may be going on.

The first line of defense that you as a good parent may have equipped your child with is the right to question authority in a respectful way. Now some of what is being taught is cut and dried facts that there is no reason to question. We know algebra works, basic physics have been proven and history, for the most part, is history.

But there are other subjects that are more speculative. Much has been made in the last few years of subjects or approaches to subjects that have been promoted at public schools that amount to opinion or a political or religious orientation that is not the school's right or responsibility to promote. So if you have taught your child they have the right to disagree with opinion or speculative teaching and they get in trouble for disagreeing with the school authorities, you are well within your rights to come to their defense.

Schools do attempt to keep parents out of the daily operation of the school simply because to have hundreds of parents getting involved in the classrooms would be chaos. And when we turn out kids over to the school to conduct classes, the implied contract is that we will give them the leverage to conduct those classes without us getting underfoot.

But that does not pass all of your rights as a parent to control both the environment of where your child will spend the day and the slant that the school may be putting on the teaching that is taking place. You have the right to be an active parent and look over the books and the syllabus of what your child is being taught. You have a right to know if what is being taught is grounded in fact or is theory and speculation so you can monitor if there is any "indoctrination", however subtle, that is taking place.

The public schools will resist your efforts to stay informed and to exercise your right to know what is going on down there. They do that based on the faulty assumption that you have no alternatives. But you do have choices. You can always take your child out of public schools who are overstepping their rights and put them in private schools who will respect your wishes, your viewpoints and the rights of your children to a good education based on facts, not opinions and conjecture.

So let's keep in mind that we do have resources to turn to if the school our children are in will not take parents rights into consideration. By using good old market pressure on the schools, we can keep them honest and doing a good job for our kids.

On Not Letting School Administrators Push You Around:

If you have found yourself outraged, frustrated and feeling a little paranoid about guiding how your child is educated in public school, don't be surprised because you are not alone. In fact, the only parents that don't have this sensation are the ones who send their kids blindly off to public school with little concern about what is being taught there and accept the curriculum without question because it's "what they are teaching at school."

Perhaps at one time such blind acceptance of authority was considered noble. But this generation is not the kinds to simply accept that just because the school administration is a public institution, then they will always make the right decisions about how to educate our children. In fact, the very fact that public schools are government functions makes you suspicious that more likely than not they are making the wrong decisions and some amount of parental oversight is called for.

The problem comes with the amount of leverage that parents actually have over public schools. And that amount of leverage is somewhere very close to zero. School administrators have parents in a spot and they know it. The public school system is set up in such a way that other than for the purposes of public opinion, schools don't have to answer to parents at all.

Now just think about what that means. You take your precious children every day and turn them over to other adults for six to eight hours of day during which those adults are given the job of putting knowledge in your child's head. But there is no accountability for what they teach and if you determine that the school is abusing the privilege of caring for your child, except if it's a criminal situation, you have no power to stop or change it.

There is no other situation in society quite like this one. And especially in this era of child abuse and our concern about the influence of others over our children, we continue to think nothing of the carte blanche power public schools have over the minds of our kids. So what can we do?

Well the ultimate vote is our presence in the system. We don't have to submit to arrogance or tyranny if that is what we see happening in our public schools. The public schools are funded by the number of students in the school. So if you simply reduce that number by one or the number of children you have and take them to private school, not only do you capture a lot of control back, you send a clear message to public schools that they are not completely outside the parental control and judgment.

Now we can only vote one family at a time. But if your public school system is abusing their privileges and not regarding your desires as parents, public outcry can raise the alarm and send a message to other parents that maybe its time for a mass exodus to private school. The threat of this kind of parent revolt is exactly what public school administrators don't want to see happen.

They would love it if we would all be good public school parents and just send cookies and never meddle in what they are doing with our children's minds. But they are accountable to you and the leverage of your participation is powerful and will cause them to pay attention. It might take some media coverage, some citizens meetings in your living room and some organization but the system will respond if you care enough to make them listen. And even if they don't private schools are paid to listen so that might be a perfectly acceptable alternative as well.

When Schools Turn into Spies

What do you pay the school to do for your child? You pay the school to educate your child. You pay them to teach them the fundamental skills in life such as mathematics, history, language, logical thinking, public speaking, government and civic responsibility and perhaps in the arts as well. Of course, when it comes to public schools, we don't pay them directly. But you pay taxes that eventually goes toward keeping the schools operational and paying the administrators and teachers.

So, even though with the government is standing in the middle of the relationship, the schools fundamentally work for you. But somehow over time, things have gotten turned around and schools have taken it upon themselves to be the bosses and judges of society and even of the parents of the children who attend the schools.

It all starts with resentment. Schools very commonly not only develop a dislike for parents, they devise elaborate systems to keep things from you and to keep you out of the business of running the school. You know the feeling you get when you come to parent teacher conferences or, God forbid, you start poking your nose into what is going on at your child's school. The message is delivered to you quite strongly to go away and leave the running of the school to the administrators and teachers and quit asking so many questions.

If this all doesn't seem just a little insidious to you, it should. When you hear horror stories about bad people who seduce children or young people, one of the first lies they tell the children is that what is going on is "our little secret so don't tell your parents." Well, that is the same message your children are getting from the schools that take care of them and if you start poking your nose into what is happening at school, you are blocked from getting very far.

But if that wasn't bad enough, public schools also take it upon themselves to pry into the private lives and the moral, ethical and religious values of your kids. Of the many reasons why the private school movement in this country has taken off so strongly, this is one of the biggest causes of people pulling kids out of public schools. Somehow, the public schools have started a practice of turning children against their parents and even using children to spy on the parents under the context of trying to flush out child abuse. They turn children into little reporters so if you discipline your child in any way, that can get back to the school who can find a way to call it child abuse and take over the situation.

The situation is nothing short of criminal. Part of the blame is a governmental system that is functioning outside of its authority attempting to control the lives and behavior of private citizens. And part of the blame is that dislike and disrespect schools have of parents. At some point along the way, the public schools decided, even if they never say so, that the kids belong to them and that parents are the enemy.

We have at our disposal ways to shut down government spying being done through the schools and through our own children. And that way is to take out kids out of public schools and put them in private schools that have respect for parents and live under parental authority, not the other way around. And if we will take advantage of this resource, public schools may get the message that they work for us and they better learn to live under that authority or they can be shut down too.

Who Holds The Schools Accountable?

Perhaps the biggest difference between public and private school is the system of accountability. Children know all about being held accountable. Not long after they leave behind infancy, children learn that virtually everybody is going to hold them accountable for something or another in almost every situation they will be in. And they become little experts at meeting the expectations of adults, even if it's just surface fulfillment of the requirements and not a genuine accountability.

But the truth is that all of us are held accountable to fulfill our responsibilities. Jobs hold employees accountable. In marriage, the husband and wives hold each other accountable to live up to the marriage vows. Even businesses are held accountable by customers. If the business fails to live up to the expectation of the customers, they will go out of business and not make any money any more.

Responsibility and accountability are the core values of what makes us tick as people and by extension what makes institutions work the way they are supposed to work to serve the needs of the public. Accountability means that someone somewhere is going to judge you on your performance. If you are performing well, you are rewarded. If you are not performing well, you are punished, corrected or dismissed. It's not a hard system to understand and your children understand it in depth.

In school, children are held accountable every day. Not only do they have to live up to behavior expectations in class, they must participate in lessons, be part of lesson related activities and do homework and take tests and get good grades to be rewarded with a high grade average to take on to the next grade and eventually to college.

But who holds the schools accountable to do the jobs they are required to do? This is the fundamental difference between public and private schools. Private schools are quite simply held accountable by the parents of the children who attend that school. Now in every private school, there is an internal system and structure to execute accountability on a daily basis in the form of the school administration and the principle. But ultimately if the school is not living up to the promises it makes to the parents who pay what are often high fees for that education for their children, those parents can pull their kids out and go elsewhere.

So a private school lives under the laws of the marketplace which keeps other businesses working correctly. They can be fired by parents so it pays for them to listen to parents, to keep parents informed and to make sure that at the end of the semester, the quality of education and the educational experience the kids had was top notch.

Public schools on the other hand are not held accountable by parents. They are held accountable by the government. And as we all know from watching how well our politicians behave, the government is pretty awful at holding anybody accountable for anything. So the public school systems and the schools in your town learn quickly how to "just get by" on satisfying government requirements and those requirements have precious little to do with the educational experience of your child or of your expectations as parents.

Now the public schools will put on a pretty good show that they want the input of parents and that they want to be accountable to parents. That is because you as a parent have two very potent weapons at your disposal that can hurt the school if they don't convince you that they are living up to expectations. You can vote and use politics to make the government live up to its job. Or you can take your child out of the public schools and take them to a school that will be responsive to your needs and expectations.

One system is bureaucratic and based on government oversight which almost never works. The other is based on the laws of the marketplace and driven by satisfying consumer need. That system is the private school system and the consumer is you and your child. And while the private school route is more expensive, by patronizing the system that works and that will be ultimately accountable to you, you are voting that the public system doesn't work so maybe someday the government will fix it. But we aren't holding our breath for that.

Protecting Your Child's Love Of Learning

Sometimes for parents who see their children come home from public school angry and antagonistic to school work and learning, we naturally assume that it is against the nature of a child to want to learn anything. But if you think back to the years before you sent your little one off to school, the opposite was the case. As an infant, your child was a virtually learning machine and he or she seemed to live and breathe learning new things. That natural curiosity and desire to find out more about the world was as deeply a part of your little one's being as the desire for food and love.

85

So what happened? Does the love of learning die out when a child passes out of infancy? Actually, if you watch your young child or teenager closely, the love of learning is still there. But what has happened is because public schools destroy the zeal for learning at an academic level, children channel their enthusiasm for learning into venues that understand the mind of youth better than schools do it seems. That is why video games and television are so successful. It isn't that these tools of communication succeed just because the things they talk about are fun. They succeed because they nurture and encourage a love of exploration and learning in ways the public schools long ago forgot (or never knew) how to do.

There is a tragic paradox to public school. The paradox is that they are charged with the highest calling in society which is to educate our youth. When we turn our children over to them, they have a tremendous opportunity to capture that zeal for learning and take it year by year forward so the child never ceases being fascinated by knowledge and the love of gaining more of it.

But sadly, almost without exception, public schools squander this golden opportunity to take young minds brimming with the thrill of learning and take them further and further never damaging the precious enthusiasm they have for knowing new things. Instead, within a short time after starting public school, your child will lose his or her love of learning and become angry, bitter and resentful of the school and of you for sending him there.

Part of the reason for this failure comes from the fact that public schools by law must handle a huge amount of children. So to maintain order, extensive crowd control and discipline systems are put in place. Somewhere along the way, schools abandon their core principle which is to teach young minds and to nurture their love of knowledge and they exchange that for order, discipline and the ability to follow rules.

Children are not stupid. They can see that the institution is not at all interested in academics and is all about order and keeping everybody marching in a line and they turn against the school. But then the schools even rob the classroom of time to subject children to hour after hour of "ethical training" in anti drug, anti sex and anti discrimination assemblies and lesson plans.

Somewhere along the way, someone saw that schools represent an unsupervised concentration of children who had time that could be monopolized to preach an ethical lesson to them. By unsupervised we mean that the parents aren't there to object. So large segments of the school day are wasted on teaching the children to be good citizens, moral people and to have "self esteem" which has only become damaged because the schools destroyed the children's love of learning in the first place.

Whether or not public schools can see how badly they have failed in their prime reason for existing or not isn't your problem as a parent. Your problem is to find a place that can rekindle the love of learning in your child and begin to move him or her along toward academic excellence so your little one knows the joy of knowledge and the thrill of excelling at learning again. The deep desire of parents to make this type of education available to their kids is the reason for the explosion of the private school movement in the last few decades. And is a movement that may become a wholesale revolution if public schools continue to destroy the minds and souls of the children they are supposed to be teaching.

Teaching Subjects or Teaching Students

Teaching school is as much a calling as it is a job. And in fact when you review the teachers at the school where your child will be going, you will notice that the good ones are as much missionaries with a zeal for guiding young minds as they are people who come to work to perform a function. But there can be no question that what makes any school great whether it's the most expensive private school in town or a public school with overcrowded classes is the quality of the teachers who will be with your child for hours each and every day.

For a teacher, deciding whether to go the public or private school route can be a tough decision. While the environment of every school is different, the calling of each teacher might be somewhat different. For teachers with a specific focus such as in music or art, to teach in a private school devoted to that niche of education is ideal. But many teachers seek to educate young people in a general area of knowledge such as math or English feel called to teach but the subject matter isn't as crucial. And for this type of teacher who thrives on larger classes and on taking disinterested students and transforming them into devout scholars, the public school setting is a good choice.

For parents evaluating schools, if you sit in on classes and are able to watch teachers work with their students, you can learn a lot just seeing that interaction and observing the body language of the teacher and how they present themselves to the class. Much of the confidence and sense of creative presentation that comes from the best teachers reflects the relationship between the school itself and the teacher.

Many times in a public school situation teachers can become so burdened with rules and stipulations that come down from the state and pertain to student behavior, safety guidelines and other non academic items that, while important, can dilute the pure relationship between teacher and subject and student.

So if you see a teacher who is having success establishing rapport with the students and engaging them with personality and humor in the subject at hand, you may be witnessing a public school administration that made it a point to make the purpose of each classroom to be about education and that is reflected in teacher attitudes as well. This is rare in the public school arena, but it happens.

This is not to say that every private school is staffed 100% with creative and inspiring teachers. So it's a good idea to evaluate several teachers in any school because, as in any profession, there are good ones and bad ones. One question you can ask while observing any teacher in action might be, "Is this teacher teaching the subject or teaching students." The difference is the attitude that teacher has toward students. Teachers who love their subject and are just looking for loyal students to absorb their wisdom do not interact with the young people as much.

But teachers who are true educators are fascinated with the learning process in students and love the interaction between student and teacher. You can tell if the instructor likes students and the affection is two ways by watching the body language of teacher and students. If there is a lot of eye contact, frequent smiling and laughter and there is a genuine joy in the room, which is a teacher who was put on this earth to be doing this one task.

And that is the kind of teacher you want your child to learn from.

While you are more likely to encounter this kind of teacher in the private school setting, these are the real gems that make any school they work in great. But if you find one particular school where this is the kind of teacher you meet the most as you review classes, that reflects that in addition to teachers who are all about education and all about making great students, you have also found a school that from the administration on down is devoted to taking young people and making them wonderful scholars and lovers of knowledge. And when you find that school, make it your child's home because that is the place to be.

Reading, Writing and Arithmetic

There seem to be a lot of reasons for sending your child to public school depending on who you talk to. From the kid's perspective, school is a chance to get out of the house and maybe have some fun with friends. And one of the values of sending a child to a social setting for school rather than going the home school route is it gives your child the chance to develop social skills which are almost as valuable as the academics.

But when it comes right down to it, for most parents, the central reason to send a child to school is for them to learn the basics of the subjects being taught which includes history, art, government, social studies, foreign language and yes reading, writing and arithmetic. If the school is successful at this one task, then anything else is secondary or lower on the priority list. Not only do you want your child to come out of each class with a good grade which builds up a good GPA in preparation for college, you want your kiddo to come out with a mastery of the subject. And if they can come out with a love or passion for each subject area, that is a tremendous bonus.

This is why it is maddening how little public school seems to focus on teaching. You can go to a parent's assembly or parent conference and go for much if not all of the meeting and hear nothing about the basics of the academics of what is going on at that school. In fact, if you dare to interrupt such a meeting to talk about the actual mission of school which is to give the children education in subjects, you often feel like you just introduced some form of obscenity to the discussion.

The emphasis in public school is far too often on behavior, conformity to the structure of school or on moral or ethical "lessons" the school likes to teach. The notifications you get from the school about your child are almost always about behavior and conformity and if you talk to the "teachers" at public schools, this is where their passion lies. It's as though the challenge of keeping 20-30 wild students tame and working within the structure of the school system has become the passion of the school far more than teaching students the subjects at hand is.

The sad thing is a lot of the time, the schools can distract parents and even students to where each and every day the entire focus of being in school is about obeying the system. Children are the first to notice that they seem enslaved to a system designed to only teach them how to be enslaved to the system.

To break this cycle of wasting your child's time on discipline and conformity training, private school is often the best route. The very reason may private schools spring into existence comes from the frustration parents have felt about getting the public schools to provide real education for their kids. So by establishing a private school, the founders made it a priority that the classes would be about teaching and about enabling students to learn and excel at academics.

What a relief it would be if when your child came home from school and you asked "what went on at school today?" you got a laundry list of academic areas of focus that your child is being taken into by the teachers of her school. This would be a breath of fresh air after hearing daily moaning about the discipline and lectures public schools give your kids with no interest in academics at all. And if we can find a school that goes back to that core value of reading, writing and arithmetic, that would be a school sending your child to go to every day, even if it is a greater cost. It's worth it if your child is really learning and if the school is actually doing its job of teaching.

Interviewing Schools

You are an adult. And when adults make big decisions in life, they have good reasons. And deciding whether to send your child to a private school and which private school to pick is a big decision. So the logical and organized way to go about finding out whether the move is a good one and what private school to pick, the adult thing to do is make a list of things you require of a private school and turn that list into your "interview questions" that you will use when you go from school to school looking for the perfect place for your child.

One way to get your list of questions developed is to list what is making you turn away from public school. After all, public school is, at least in theory, free so to turn from a free educational resource to one you have to pay for, you need good reasons. Some of the most common reasons people consider private over public schools include:

- o   Quality of education.

- o   College preparation.

- o Accommodation for children with special needs.

- o Accommodation for children with exceptional talents.

- o School violence or drugs.

- o Public school overemphasis on moral and ethical teaching.

- o Public school sex education programs.

- o School security to prevent mass shootings like happened at Columbine.

There are other reasons to consider private school in addition to our short list. The problem is that public school does not have the leverage nor are they interested in making any changes if you do have issues with the school. Parents and students are expected to pretty much just put up with the way it is. And that drives lots of parents to look elsewhere for educational options.

The next level of focus after the areas of improvement you want from public school pertain to any specific needs you need for your child or your family that would narrow down your search for a good private school. If one of the big goals is to find a private school where your child can continue to grow in your faith, then you will only look at schools that focus on that niche.

You may have a child who is developmentally or physically challenged. There are some outstanding schools that can help with that need far better than public school. Or you may have a child who is exceptional in some particular area such as the performing arts, academics or science. Magnet schools or schools designed to give your child the additional help to move ahead more quickly in their field of specialization are an outstanding choice for you.

In all cases, you will want to interview the school as to how the school day takes place, what makes the lifestyle your child will experience at their school superior to public school and how they handle basics like nutrition, medical needs and security. These interview questions go beyond just asking the administration questions and will call for you to take a tour and interview different support departments in the school.

Finally, don't overlook letting your child add some questions to the check list. After all, this school will be your child's home away from home. She may want to know how often the school has dances or field trips to break up the classroom setting. She may need to understand lunch hour or how the library works. Include in your interview a complete tour of the school which might include sitting in on some classes that your child would become a part of to watch the teachers in action.

You can tell a lot about the level of affection between teachers and students watching them teach and then observing them in the halls as they interact with the kids. And if the teachers like the kids, you know they are happy teaching there and they are doing a good job. Moreover, a warm relationship between the staff and the student body reflects that the administration of the school has designed everything from the school layout to the curriculum to how discipline is handled to work with the students and to work for their ultimate good rather than treating them like enemies as happens too often in public school. So use all of your senses when evaluating a new school so you come home with a good idea if this is the perfect next step in your child's academic career.

Conclusion

It was not that long ago when children's education was limited by geographical boundaries and local school districts. More and more, the government is working to offer parents more of a choice when it comes to the school in which they enroll their children. The option to enroll your child in the school of your choice is available no matter where you live, just as long as a sufficient amount of space is available in the classrooms.

This alteration in school enrollment provides more opportunities to many students. However, with so many options, it is more important than ever for parents to take the time to do their homework. A sufficient amount of research must be done in order to determine which school is right for your child.

The educational options, from public schools to private schools, seem overwhelmingly endless. Nonetheless, it is important to keep in mind that finding the right school should be less about the schools available and more about the needs of your child. Begin researching by visiting some of the websites online that specialize in profiling schools. Find schools that meet your criteria to narrow your list. This will make the process of evaluating schools in your area much easier and incredibly less time consuming.

In order to narrow down your list of possible schools, you need to identify the ideal educational environment for your child. The three main factors that you need to consider, as we have learned in the previous chapters of this book, are your personal expectations as a parent, your child's preferences and desires and schools that have the ability to deliver both.

The expectations that you have for your child will vary according to age. Most of the time, the children are most concerned with the extracurricular activities and the size of the school. It is up to the parents to focus on things that are more important such as test scores, educational styles and academic rankings.

As discussed earlier in this book, the most important questions that you need to ask about each school on your list include:

- Is this school and accredited institution? If so, by whom?

- How does this particular school rank academically?

- Is there a tuition fee to attend this school? If so, what is the total cost of tuition for an entire year?

- Are the classes available at this school on the same educational level as your child's ability to learn?

- Does this school provide an environment that is more nurturing or more competitive?

- Are any specific religious or educational philosophies followed?

- Does this school follow a progressive or traditional curriculum?

- Where is the location of the school campus? What are your options for transportation and what fees are required for available services?

- What are the demographics of this particular school?

- What are the requirements for graduation?

- What percentages of students graduate from this particular school? How many of those students go on to attend college?

In addition to your own desires and expectation for the new school, the needs and expectations of your child are also important to finding a school at which they will be able to grow and thrive academically. More often than not, the success or failure of a child in a particular educational environment can be attributed for the most part to their happiness, or the lack of happiness, at school.

Children will be most attracted to the schools that offer activities that appeal to their own hobbies and interests. They are interested in the schools that provide classes in their favorite subjects. In addition, most students are concerned with the size of the student body as well as the student-teacher ratio. Students want to know just what the teachers at each institution would expect from them.

Your son or daughter may also be interested in finding a school that offers art, music, sports or many other activities in which they can participate. In addition, they may also prefer a school where their friends attend.

Once you have narrowed down the number of schools on your list, it is time to consider paying a visit to the most favorable schools in your area. In addition to meeting with the teachers and school administrators, you will also be able to observe a class in session to determine which school is the right one for your child. Even when a school looks good on paper, you may be surprised by what you find out on an actual visit to the campus.

Do not be shocked if when all is said and done the school that turns out to be the right one for your son or daughter is not the one with the highest academic ranking or the best test scores. The best school for your child is going to be the one that

101

provides him or her with everything that they need academically in a nurturing environment in which they can grow and prosper.

Many, many parents all around the world have spent many long hours trying to determine the best ways to improve the chances of their child receiving the best possible education. However, instead of focusing on raising standards and improving teacher training, which are factors that distinguish the most effective schools from the poorest; the powers that be have decided that the public school system is broken beyond repair. Many government officials believe that all different types of students should be awarded vouchers that will allow them to attend religious or private schools at the taxpayers' expense.

Although such belief is quite widespread, it fails to hold up to cautious scrutiny. In fact, studies indicate that the quality of the education that is available to children varies greatly within all different school categories. Both private schools as well as the public school system contain schools with excellent academic ranking and a high rate of graduates entering respectable universities. On the other hand, you will also find both public and private school across the country that is horrible institutions with nothing valuable to offer your child.

Recently, a controversial report was released by the United States Department of Education that showed a comparison among private and public school in terms of the students' academic achievement. The report measured the educational progress of students across the country based on the federal reading and math tests, which is part of the National Assessment of Educational Progress.

This study, just like others in the past, discredited the theory that private schools are undeniably superior to their public counterparts. The study shows that private schools seem to have students with higher achievements when only the students' raw scores were considered. However, those apparent advantages seemed to melt away when variables such as gender, race, household income and parent education was taken into account by the researchers.

It cannot be stressed enough that you must keep your child's specific needs and desires as one of the main deciding factors when you enroll them in a new school. It does not make any difference if your child is just starting school as a preschooler, moving up from primary to middle school or changing schools for some reason during high school. Your child is the person who will be expected to sit in the classrooms of the school you choose for up to eight hours a day, five days a week. It is crucial that he or she is comfortable and happy in their learning environment.

As a parent, it is important to talk to your son or daughter about the things that make them happy or sad, especially while they are at school. Set aside some time to talk to your child before you make your final decision on a new school. Discuss any problems that your child has had at previous schools or with any academic issues they feel may hold them back in a fast-paced environment.

It is always good to talk with the other parents and grandparents in the area, especially if your family is moving to a new neighborhood. Ask which schools their children and grandchildren attend. You should also find out whether their experience with that particular school has been favorable. Remember when you visit the schools of your choice that you request to sit in a class and talk with some of the students, this will give you a valuable inside view of each school. You will be able to experience some of what your son or daughter will be expected to endure each and every day at the school you choose.

Once you have done all of the homework necessary in researching to find the school that is best for your child, you should have an abundance of data collected. Take the time to review all of the information that you have compounded. Once you are able to narrow the choices down to no more than four schools, get together with your child to discuss all of the options available at each institution. You should also take your child with you to the most favorable schools on your list before enrollment. Most children are able to tell right away if they feel as if they would be on the outs at a particular school.

Simply choosing private or public is not all there is to selecting the ideal school for your child. No one knows better than you do what is best for your child. Take the time to follow through with all of the steps that you have learned in this book in order to determine the specific educational needs of your child. Be sure to keep your list of questions with you at all times. After you visit each of the schools with your child, always remember to ask what he or she thought about the prospective school.

Looking to get your hands on more great books?

Come visit us on the web and check out our great collection of books covering all categories and topics. We have something for everyone.

http://www.kmspublishing.com

Made in the USA
Lexington, KY
15 February 2018